PREVENTION AND CONTINGENCIES

STEVE KING

PREVENTION AND CONTINGENCIES
A Simple Guide to Process Management

PREVENTION AND CONTINGENCIES
A SIMPLE GUIDE TO PROCESS MANAGEMENT

iUniverse books may be ordered through booksellers or by contacting:

iUniverse
1663 Liberty Drive
Bloomington, IN 47403
www.iuniverse.com
1-800-Authors (1-800-288-4677)

Because of the dynamic nature of the Internet, any web addresses or links contained in this book may have changed since publication and may no longer be valid. The views expressed in this work are solely those of the author and do not necessarily reflect the views of the publisher, and the publisher hereby disclaims any responsibility for them.

Any people depicted in stock imagery provided by Getty Images are models, and such images are being used for illustrative purposes only. Certain stock imagery © Getty Images.

ISBN: 978-1-6632-0446-2 (sc)
ISBN: 978-1-6632-0445-5 (e)

Library of Congress Control Number: 2020912300

Print information available on the last page.

iUniverse rev. date: 07/24/2020

From the author of *Six Conversations* and *Alignment, Process, and Relationships*

The Process of Process Management

3

Of course, process management is itself a process. In its simplest form, it is a seven-step process:

1. Know the process.
2. Set the standards.
3. Know the acceptable variances from standards.
4. Have a reporting mechanism for tracking variances.
5. Install preventative and contingency measures.
6. Analyze the performance data regularly.
7. If negatively off variance, execute the contingency plans.

In the following chapters, we'll explore each of these steps and equip you with the basic tools needed to manage your processes well. Let me take a moment here to give you a few words of introduction about each of these seven steps.

Know the process means understanding each step in the process. The way we build this understanding is by having those who execute the process map it. You've no doubt seen process maps or process diagrams. These give us a visual representation of how the process unfolds and allows anyone, even those who are not part of executing the process, a quick way to get familiar with it.

Set the standards means establishing what success looks like when the process is properly executed. There are standards for each step and standards for the whole process.

Know the acceptable variances from standards is an acknowledgment that acceptable standards for a process are often a range of acceptability. If the process operates within the range, good. If the process operates outside the range, there might be a problem with delivering the desired result. A manager needs to know what is acceptable.

Have a reporting mechanism for tracking variances suggests some kind of report needs to be available to the manager so he or she can identify any unacceptable process variances. The report can come in a variety of forms—verbal, paper, or electronic. Any reporting must be timely in order to be acted on before a process fails.

Install preventative and contingency measures refers to ways a manager can handle foreseen problems with the

> "Preventative and contingency measures keep a process on track."

process. A foreseen problem can either be prevented before it happens, with a preventative step or measure installed as a remedy, or, if it cannot easily be prevented, a contingency measure should be installed to be executed if the problem rears its head. Preventative and contingency measures keep a process on track. They are the key to process management.

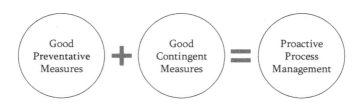

Analyze the performance data regularly refers to the established routine of using the reporting mechanisms.

Execute the contingency plans is the planned—just in case—action prepared for when a foreseen problem happens. It's putting the backup plan in motion and is triggered when a reported variance is negative or is expected to have a negative impact on the outcome of the process.

I'll be emphasizing throughout the book that process management is a team sport. While I think the manager is the accountable party for various processes, his or her team members are typically closest to various parts of those processes. To really *know the process*, for example, an entire team should participate in the mapping or diagraming of the process. The benefit of team collaboration is twofold. First, the manager gets the benefit of insights from those actually doing the work. Second, the manager can use the exercise of a team-mapping process as a way for each team member to see the whole process and his or her part in it. This big picture can provide some employees greater motivation to get their parts of the process done right, since they can see the downstream impact of their work.

4

Know the Process ... and
How Many You Own

In my introduction, I mentioned that when I ask managers how many processes they own, many of those managers have a problem answering the question. So, we need to start there.

How many processes do you own? Uncertain? Here are some ways to determine what you are being held responsible for:

1. Ask your boss, which seems like the quickest way to get some clarity.
2. Look at your performance goals. Whatever processes are central to you achieving those goals are probably processes that you either own or co-own.
3. Consider who your customers are. These can be either internal or external customers. What products and/or services are you delivering to these customers? The work activities you use to deliver those products and services are probably processes you own.
4. Think about processes you own at the team level, meaning not individual work activities owned by each individual member of your team but rather processes that are likely touched by the work activities of more than one member of the team.

I would like to emphasize the importance of that fourth point, since it calibrates the level of process detail a manager needs to manage. All work can be broken down into steps. And sometimes each of those steps can be broken down into more steps. This might lead a manager to believe he or she owns and manages seventy-five different processes, and that is an overwhelming thought.

My first manager job was as the head of professional development at a bank of about four thousand employees. In that role, I felt my team and I owned five processes:

1.   A process for assessing the development needs of the bank's professional ranks

2.   A process for designing and developing training programs

3.   A process for delivering the instruction

4.   A process for administering course enrollment

5.   A process for evaluating the effectiveness of the training

Each of these processes had subprocesses that had subprocesses. But when I looked at the expectations of my customers (who were all internal), considered my performance goals, and saw what results I was being held accountable for, these five processes were probably the best distillation of what I truly owned. If I managed these five processes well and my team executed on those processes well, things were good.

How many processes will a typical frontline manager own? The answer seems to be between three and seven. So, I recommend you look at those customer expectations and performance goals, look at the work being done by your team, do a little commonsense distillation, and name no more than seven processes to focus your management attention on.

Once you have done that, you can turn to defining the details of each of those processes. The best way to know a process is to have personally done each process step repeatedly. Some managers have this kind of personal experience with their processes, which helps a lot. The second-best way to know a process is to have those who handle the various steps share what they do and illustrate it as a process map or diagram.

I imagine you have seen process maps before. They come in all sorts of shapes and sizes. Some are very high level; others are quite detailed. Just to make sure we are talking about the same thing, here is an example of a process map, this one depicting the expected steps in a visit to a doctor's office.

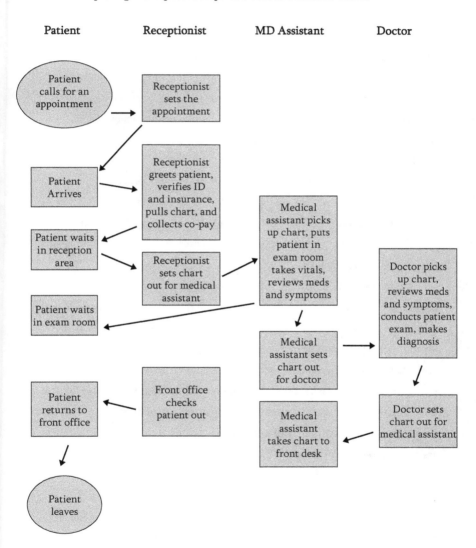

It is not my objective in this small book to teach the ins and outs of developing a process map. There are plenty of excellent resources on the web you can tap for that. But there are a few suggestions I would like to make.

First, include the entire team in the mapping activity. Those working the process know it the best. Plus, it helps team members gain a sense of how their work fits into the larger picture.

> "Those working the process know it the best."

Second, start by focusing on mapping the steps in the process and don't worry about standards, metrics, or acceptable variance. That can come later.

Third, if you happen to have access to decent process-mapping software, use it. But honestly, for the first draft, Post-it notes and an empty wall will do just fine.

Fourth, put some time between the first draft of the process map and the final draft. I have found that a little reflection time between drafts often brings additional insights and subsequent useful adjustments to the final map.

Fifth and lastly, try to build a map that represents a level of detail that is useful as a management tool.

Let me expand on this last point. For our doctor's visit, one version of the process map might have been this: (1) patient arrives, (2) MD sees patient, and (3) patient leaves. Yes, that is a process. It has three steps and a beginning and an end. But it is not useful to a manager trying to manage it. It is at too high a level. At the other extreme, the step under the column titled "Medical Assistant" that states "medical assistant sets chart out for doctor" could be further broken down into this: (1) medical assistant picks up chart, (2) medical assistant opens door, (3) medical assistant walks down the hall to exam room, (4) medical assistant places chart on desk in exam room, and (5) medical assistant returns to his or her office. Here we have details unimportant to managing the process. It is too detailed.

The goal is to understand a process at a level that can highlight key steps that, if they go awry, will hinder efficiency and effectiveness. Mapping to this appropriate level of understanding is a little more art than science. Trust your instincts and the instincts of your team. If you don't find that sweet spot in your first iteration, you'll know it as you actually start managing key steps in the process, and you can then return to the mapping exercise and make some adjustments.

Standards and Variances

5

Once a process has been visually mapped, it is time to layer in our understanding of the standards our process must meet and what kind of variances from those standards are acceptable.

All processes have at least one customer. These customers have expectations about the product or service they will receive when the process is complete. We'll call those expectations the *customer standards*. All processes are made up of steps, and each step needs to be done properly. Each step will have an expected standard as well—one that defines successful completion of a step. We'll call those expectations *input standards*.

Let's get better acquainted with standards and variances by looking at another example. This next map depicts a basic recruiting process. The customer is a hiring manager. The process owner is whoever owns the hiring process. In many organizations, that would be HR. But in plenty of smaller businesses, that process ownership might land on an administrative assistant or someone else.

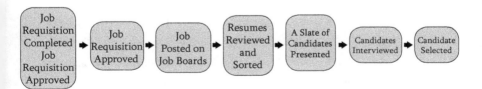

The customer (hiring manager) standard here might be something such as *new person hired within thirty business days at a direct cost of no more than $500.* Each of those seven steps in the process will have its own input standard. Here are what those input standards might look like.

1. **Job requisition completed.** Requisition form filled out properly by the hiring manager.

2. **Job requisition approved.** Hiring manager's boss signs requisition form indicating approval within three days of receiving the form.

3. **Jobs posted on job boards.** Recruiter selects the appropriate job board and posts the job within one day of receiving approval for the requisition. The cost of the posting must not exceed $200.

4. **Résumés reviewed and sorted.** Recruiter reviews and sorts existing and new résumés to find the best candidates for the job within a week of posting the jobs on the job boards.

5. **Slate of candidates presented.** Recruiter offers the top three to five candidates to the hiring manager for their consideration within a day of completing the review and sorting step. The manager accepts, rejects, or edits the slate. If the slate is accepted or edited, the process continues. If the slate is rejected, the recruiter returns to step 3.

6. **Candidates interviewed.** Recruiter sets up the interview schedule with candidates and interviewers within one week of getting an acceptable slate. The scheduling and interviews are completed over ten business days. The cost of interview expenses must not exceed $300.

7. **Candidate selected.** Manager selects the candidate to hire within one day of completing the interviews. The recruiter offers the candidate the role within one day of getting the manager's choice. If the job is accepted, the process is complete. If the job is rejected, the manager selects another candidate to offer the job. If all acceptable candidates reject the job, the recruiter returns to step 3.

Setting all these standards can be tedious work, but it is an essential part of process management. You can't address prevention and contingencies without clear standards. Start with the customer standards. Then back into the input standards to ensure the customer gets what he or she needs. In this case, the aggregate time frames and costs laid out in the input standards must meet or be less than the customer standard of the hiring managers—*a new hire within thirty business days at a direct cost of less than $500.*

> "You can't address prevention and contingencies without clear standards."

What if the customer of the process is asking for a standard to be met that is simply not doable? Yes, some customers are unreasonable. For example, a hiring manager might say he or she wants a slate within one day of the requisition being completed. That would be unreasonable. This is where a process owner's advocacy skills will be tested. Sometimes process owners and customers must negotiate standards. In the next chapter, I'll give some tips on how to handle this situation.

Variances to standard are simply a measure of how closely the process reflects the expected standard.

In our example, if the interview schedule is completed in only five business days, that would be a positive variance. On the other hand, if the interview schedule took fifteen days to complete, that would be a negative variance. Any step in which there is a regular negative variance should be considered a target for some preventative or contingency measures. We'll talk about those measures in a later chapter. Any step in which there is a regular positive variance should be considered for an adjustment to standard and therefore an improvement to the productivity of that process.

In my example, the input standards were set as a single metric such as "within ten business days" or "up to $300." In some processes, acceptable standards are set like a range. It might be something such as "at a cost between $200 and $400." This is often the case when the process differs a bit with each iteration. In our example, perhaps different kinds of hires might require more money spent on certain specialty job boards. The range accounts for this difference and allows for variations to single iterations of the process if the customer standards are met, as an average, over some agreed-upon period—let's say a year.

A well-run process would not have many positive or negative variances to standard, since one is an indication that the process is suboptimizing its potential, and the other is an indication that the process is not meeting expectations.

Decision Rights and Process Management

6

In my book *Alignment, Process, and Relationships*, I highlighted the need to clarify ownership for parts of any process. I called this ownership *decision rights*. In that book, my emphasis was on specific decisions that a team would need to make. My opinion was that wherever there is a key decision to be made, a manager should make it clear who on the team gets to make that decision.

Some of you might recognize this description of decision rights as a kind of RACI analysis. RACI stands for "responsible, accountable, consulted, and informed." It is a tool that can help a manager sort out, for any given task in a process, who is responsible and accountable for the task, who must be consulted before the task is executed, and who must be informed once the task is complete. If you are unacquainted with RACI, I would suggest you search the web. There are plenty of great resources available online you can tap for more information.

I want to focus on decision rights at this point to expand a bit on the second step in the process of process management, on setting the standards. In our earlier discussion about standards, I highlighted both quantifiable standards, as in this example:

> *Jobs posted on job boards*. Recruiter selects the
> appropriate job board and posts the job within *one day* of

receiving approval for the requisition. The cost of the posting must *not exceed $200.*

And I highlighted qualitative standards, as in this example:

> *Résumés reviewed and sorted.* Recruiter reviews and sorts existing and new résumés to *find the best candidates* for the job within a week of posting the jobs on the job boards.

But what might have been taken for granted in these two examples are the decision rights. In the first example, the recruiter owns the decision rights to select the job boards he or she uses. In the second example, the recruiter owns the decision rights to select the best candidates from the pool of available résumés. Making these kinds of rights clear and explicit is important to ensuring the process unfolds as expected. Imagine if that first example had read like this:

> "Making these kinds of rights clear and explicit is important to ensuring the process unfolds as expected."

> *Jobs posted on job boards.* The appropriate job board is selected, and jobs are posted on that board within *one day* of receiving approval for the requisition. The cost of the posting must *not exceed $200.*

In this case, the decision rights are left unclear, and confusion could ensue. Perhaps the recruiter will pick the job board and post the job. Or perhaps the hiring manager will think he or she can pick the job board. Or perhaps the recruiter's manager will opt to pick the job board because he or she likes to micromanage things. Or maybe worse, no one picks a job board, and the process grinds to a halt.

Use the moment when process standards are being established to name who owns the decision rights for each step in the process. Consider it one of the standards that must be made clear.

7

Data, Experience, Assumptions … and How Much Certainty Is Needed

Before I move on to a discussion of reporting mechanisms and the installation of preventative and contingency measures, I want to take a moment to reflect on how we arrive at standards and reasonable variances.

The Process of Process Management

1. Know the process.
2. **Set the standards.**
3. **Know the acceptable variances from standards.**
4. Have a reporting mechanism for tracking variances.
5. Install preventative and contingency measures.
6. Analyze the performance data regularly.
7. If negatively off variance, execute the contingency plans.

> "Standards are not chosen out of thin air; neither are variances."

Standards are not chosen out of thin air; neither are variances. Instead, they come about primarily through a combination of three things: data, experience, and assumptions.

Several years back, I read a book titled *The Fifth Discipline Field Book: Strategies and Tools for Building a Learning Organization* by Peter Senge. In this book, Senge introduced me to a model called the "ladder of inference." This model was based on work by the famous cognitive psychologist Chris Argyris. Here is an outline version of this ladder—you read it from the bottom up.

Actions I Will Take / Decisions I Will Make

Beliefs I Adopt

Conclusion I Draw

Assumptions I Make

Meaning I Add Informed by My Personal Experience

Data I Select to Use

Data and Information I Observe

This model is useful in understanding how someone can set standards and variances for a process. It is basically a decision-making model. Let's look more carefully at it.

The top of the ladder represents an action taken—like setting process standards and acceptable variances. How is the appropriate action taken? Senge said it begins at the bottom of the ladder with data we have available to us and what data we select or choose to work with. Once we have the data, we add meaning to that data; we interpret that data. Now, the only way we can interpret data is through the lens of our own experiences. If I read data on birds and I am an ornithologist, I will see things in that data the average bird lover will not see. Experience influences meaning. If three people are interpreting the data, then you have the benefit of three experiences.

Once meaning is added, and if there are gaps in our understanding due to insufficient data or experience, and if a decision needs to be made, then we'll fill those gaps with assumptions. Assumptions are best guesses. That bird is little and yellow, and I assume it is a goldfinch. When we have only a little data about a step in the process and no serious experience with the process, assumptions often become primary means of setting a standard.

The ladder is completed with two final rungs: conclusions based on data, experience, and assumptions and beliefs formed over time. Beliefs are a particularly tricky part of this decision-making model. If someone holds a particularly strong belief, he or she will likely seek out data that supports that belief. This is called *confirmation bias* and can lead someone down an ill-chosen decision path. People might even reject data that does not conform to their beliefs. The difference between assumptions and beliefs is that assumptions can easily change with new data and new experience. Beliefs do not change quite so easily.

I am introducing the ladder of inference here so we can imagine using it to set process standards and variances. But honestly, this is a useful tool for any decisions facing you as a manager. A routine of checking your data, adding meaning to that data with a thoughtful application of your life experiences, clarifying and testing assumptions, and acknowledging beliefs is a healthy routine that I find improves manager performance and productivity. It is particularly useful in team settings where a diversity of data, experiences, assumptions, and beliefs can be leveraged to find the best solutions to problems. There are plenty of good resources about the ladder of inference on the web. If you're curious, go check some of them out.

I am guessing you see the relevance of the ladder in setting process standards and variances. First, you seek as much data that is available about the process suggesting the appropriate standards. This data might be housed in reports, process maps, policy manuals, or process logs. Be careful. The data might be good, or it might be poor. But it is where you want to start. Second, you want to tap the experiences of those who have used this process for a while. Ideally, you'll want to tap the experiences of many and hope to hear a similar story time and time again. This redundancy is a good sign you're zeroing in on agreement of possible standards. What if this is a new process, or what if this is a radically changed process? In these cases, data and experience available to set standards might be a little thin, which is when assumptions come into play. We use assumptions to fill the void. Test those assumptions with the early iterations of the process. Then change those assumptions and standards with the new data and experiences.

The recruiting process outlined in the previous chapter is a good example of a process that has plenty of data available and plenty of experience available to tap when setting standards and variances. Even if a company was starting to build a recruiting process from scratch, the benchmark data can be sourced, and most businesspeople have some hiring experience. In an earlier chapter, I mentioned that I once owned a process for evaluating the effectiveness of training. My team and I had virtually no experience with serious training evaluation, and the data available on program evaluation was not great. So, our early versions of the process and those early standards were built mostly on assumptions. For example, we assumed that if someone rated a program four or five out of five (five being the best rating and one being the worst), people were pleased with the class. That was one of our standards that needed testing over time to ensure the assumption was right.

So, how much data is enough data to set proper process standards and variances? This is a question that pivots on the issues of *risk* and *certainty*. You should look at a lot of data and tap those with plenty of relevant experience for processes at a high risk of harm if they fail. Perhaps good examples of high-risk situations are certain processes inside a nuclear power plant. The risk of failure is the possible loss of life, so the processes and related standard and variances must be nearly perfect. The standard of a four or five out of five for a training program simply does not carry the same level of risk. Setting that standard without much data to start and collecting and testing it as time goes on is probably fine. You should assess the risk factor when deciding how much data to chase down before deciding on standards.

Reporting Mechanisms— Knowing When You're on Track

8

Some managers are quite active in the processes they manage. They might be responsible for specific steps in the process. They might work in close vicinity to team members and assess, daily or hourly, if those members are meeting the expected standards. They may be in close contact with their customers and hear directly from them if those customer standards are being met. For these kinds of managers, there is probably not a great need for a formal, documented reporting mechanism. They know how the process is performing because they see processes unfold before them all the time.

Not all managers are in that close of contact with the myriad of processes they own. So, if they want to know if the process is performing, they need some kind of reporting to inform them.

In the earlier example of the simple bookkeeping process, there may be a standard to register the payment in the system within twenty-four hours of receipt.

And let's assume there are typically twenty payments received per day. The person responsible for registering the payment might, at the end of the day, simply send the manager a note indicating all twenty payments have been registered, or nineteen out of twenty were registered. This, of course, is an additional step in the process. But if the manager felt it was important to the efficacy of the process to know if all the payments were in the system within twenty-four hours, then the manager might want to add this reporting step.

Of course, it is just as likely that a payment registered into the system will have a system-generated report or dashboard that the manager can simply access without that added step. The manager might want the report "pushed" to him or her at the end of the day or the manager might simply "pull" the report or dashboard to see if the payments were registered. Whether reports are pushed or pulled depends on plenty of factors, including common/past practice, how frequent the manager needs to see data, or simply the manager's or employee's preference.

In the training evaluation process mentioned earlier, the customer standard was a score on posttraining assessment of a four or five out of five. Back in the day, someone tallied up all the paper assessments at the end of the week and left a report on my desk. Nowadays, more posttraining assessments are conducted online, and a report on the results is either pushed to or pulled by the manager for review.

> "There is no use setting standards and knowing acceptable or unacceptable variances if you don't have a way to monitor them."

There is no use setting standards and knowing acceptable or unacceptable variances if you don't have a way to monitor them. Therefore, thoughtful reporting is essential to good process management.

One word of caution: place reporting at only the key junctures of the process rather than at every step. I have seen some managers use reporting to micromanage the process and their people. There is no need to do that. Focus instead on those steps where there is a high likelihood of negative variance or process breakdowns—the topic of our next chapter.

9

Naming the Likely Breakdowns— Knowing Your Trouble Spots

One challenge facing managers who are trying to manage their processes is the task of selecting or identifying which steps in a process to attach preventative and contingency actions to. In high concept, you would have such actions for every step in a process, but that may not be necessary or even practical. Some process steps are so well honed that managers can knowingly expect them to happen without a hitch. These probably don't need a formal preventative or contingent action associated with them. Some processes have hundreds of steps, and it may not be practical to tag each step with another preventative or contingent step.

So, how does a manager pick the process's steps that are likely to cause them headaches and need a backup plan? The answer comes in a Pareto way of thinking. The Pareto principle is often known as the 80/20 rule (infrequently known as the principle of factor sparsity) and states that, for most events, roughly 80 percent of the effects come from 20 percent of the causes.

Here is a simple example of the Pareto principle in use. Let's imagine a large organization has something called a Project Management Office or PMO. This office can be contracted to handle key projects throughout the organization.

The PMO has decided its process for project management will be these six steps (yes, I know project management is more complex than six steps, but for our purposes, this truncated version will do).

1. A manager contracts for a project manager's services.

2. Project objectives and scope are established.

3. Project tasks, resources, and personnel are identified.

4. Project plan is written.

5. Project plan is implemented and monitored.

6. Project is evaluated and closed out.

Let's say the customer standards for this project work are the following:

1. All project objectives are met.

2. Project managers provide regular updates to the contracting manager.

3. Projects come in on time.

4. Projects come in on budget.

5. The project manager displays a clear understanding of the contracting manager's needs.

The Pareto principle is applied twice. First, which of the customer standards are the most important to the client? In this example, we'll say the client highlights "all project objectives met" and "projects come in on time" as the two top concerns. Second, we look at the process and ask, Which steps in the process are most likely to negatively affect achieving those key clients concerns? Here, the PMO manager, with the help of the project managers, uses data, experiences, and assumptions to determine that step 2 (project objectives and scope are established) and step 5 (project is implemented and monitored) are the most likely places in the process of project management where things could go sideways and customer needs could be unmet.

Note that we have pulled out the ladder of inference to help identify particular trouble spots in the process. Actually, the ladder has been used twice. The first is when the client determines his or her standards for success and which among them is most important. The client may or may not have given these standards a lot of thought, but he or she used the ladder knowingly or unknowingly when making his or her decisions. The second use of the ladder is when the PMO decides which process steps are worrisome when imagining meeting those client standards. Here the ladder is best used explicitly. The process manager—in this case the project manager—should be looking at any data on the process, consider his or her experiences with the process, and name clearly any assumptions and beliefs that might lead him or her to identifying those process trouble spots.

So, the recipe for finding those troubles spots in your process that become candidates for eventual preventative and contingent measures would be as follows:

o   Start with client expectations.

o   Pick out the most important of them.

o   Use those important expectations and pick out the process steps most likely to affect those expectations.

o   Stir in a generous amount of ladder of inference.

Once those process trouble spots have been located, there is one more step the process manager must take. He or she needs to answer the question, "Why does this step sometimes or often go awry?" The process manager needs to do some root-cause analysis so he or she can apply the proper preventative or contingent measure.

The science of root-cause analysis has been around for quite a while. I first ran into formal root-cause analysis in a book titled *The Rational Manager* by Kepner and Tregoe. The updated version is called *The New Rational Manager.* But much of what we call root-cause analysis was germinated in ancient Greece and China and refined by people like Edward Deming of statistical process control fame. So, as you can imagine, there are plenty of approaches, tools, and techniques a manager can draw on to clarify the root cause of a troublesome process step. The web is awash with good primers on various cause-analysis techniques. Here are a few you might investigate:

o   The Five Whys

o   Failure Mode and Effects Analysis

o   Rapid Problem Resolution

o   Fishbone Cause and Effect Diagrams

Each has its own pros and cons. I suggest you and your team take a tour of these techniques on the web and select which might work best for you.

For our purposes, let me drill down on one specific approach I will call the "what's working, what's not working" technique. I like this approach since it taps our intuitive reflex to compare elements of a situation that is working to one that is not.

The framework is simple. We start with these four questions:

1.   What is working, and what is not working?
2.   Where is it working, and where is it not working?
3.   When was it working, and when was it not working?
4.   Who was involved when it was working, and who was involved when it was not working?

Let's return to our recruiting process we looked at a few chapters back.

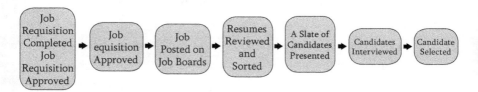

And let's imagine that the troublesome step in this process is the fifth step—the slate of candidates presented. The presenting problem with this step is that about 40 percent of the time, the slate is weak and includes no great candidate worthy of hiring. Why is this happening?

First, we ask what is working and what is not working. In this case, we'll say the previous four steps in the process are working (meeting standards), but the fifth step is not.

Second, we ask, Where is it working, and where is it not working? You ask your buddy in another part of the company if she is having problems with her slate of candidates, and she says no. So, it is not working in your part of the business, but it is elsewhere.

Third, we ask, When was it working, and when was it not working? You note that this problem with weak slates began about six months ago. Prior to that, the slates were good.

Fourth, we ask, Who was involved when it was working, and who was involved when it was not working? You are the same hiring manager, so you are a constant. You note that seven months ago, a new recruiter was assigned to you, and that recruiter expanded the list of job boards they used to create slates.

With just these four questions, we can narrow things down to two root-cause suspects: the quality of the recruiter and/or the quality of the job boards. With these in hand, you can investigate and remedy.

What if your buddy told you that she was also experiencing weak slates, and it has been happening for about seven months? In this case, the new recruiter probably moves down the list of potential causes. Upon further investigation, you find no new job boards were being used. So, the job boards move down the list of potential causes. This suggests we ask what might have happened seven months ago that would change the quality of candidate slates. Perhaps an increasingly tight job market or perhaps refusal by your company to keep up with competitive wages over the last two years has come home to roost. These become your new root-cause suspects worthy of some investigation.

This consistent comparison of what, where, when, and who are working or are not working uncovers serious root-cause candidates for you and your team to consider. Let me emphasize *team* here. Your team is likely to have a wider and deeper understanding of the process, and a particular process step, than you do as a manager, so include them in the root-cause exercise, whichever technique you end up using. Your chances of getting to that root cause improves when you do.

Principles and Process

10

Before we move on to putting the heart of proactive process management—preventative and contingent measures—into the story line, I want to have a sidebar on the notion of work based on principles instead of, or in addition to, process.

When any of us stop in at a fast-food restaurant, we know there is plenty of process that goes into fulfilling our order. But there is something else at play that guides the work, and those would be certain workplace principles.

For example, those workers who staff the counter and wait on customers are asked to be cheerful when greeting us and appreciative when they hand us our food. Workers handling the grill are expected to be careful when handling the food to ensure their and our safety.

I suppose cheerfulness could be broken down into a process step—*step 1, smile when the customer approaches*—but that is probably taking process a little too far.

Work guided by principles is relatively common. The physician's Hippocratic oath, summarized as "first do no harm," is a good example. It is not a process step but rather a guideline around which work gets done. The Institute of Management Accountants has a number of standards for ethical professional conduct. Here is one of them: "refrain from engaging in any conduct that would prejudice carrying out duties ethically." We can safely call this a work principle. The New York State Bar Association publishes what they call "ethical considerations," or ECs. Here is EC 1-7: "A lawyer should avoid bias and condescension toward, and treat with dignity and respect, all parties, witnesses, lawyers, court employees, and other persons involved in the legal process."

Work principles are kind of like guardrails. They set the boundaries of behaviors within which good work

"Work principles are kind of like guardrails."

gets done. Some work principles find their way into processes, often as input standards.

In an earlier chapter, we laid out standards for steps in the recruiting process. Here is what was said about the first step in that process:

1. **Job requisition completed**. Requisition form filled out properly by the hiring manager.

    Perhaps the recruiting manager has set a working principle of "accuracy matters," and this standard reflects that principle.

Here is standard associated with the second step in that process:

2. **Jobs posted on job boards**. Recruiter selects the appropriate job board and posts the job within one day of receiving approval for the requisition. The cost of the posting must not exceed $200.

    Perhaps this standard reflects a working principle that states, "Keep an eye on the cost of your work."

In other work situations, the principles seem to stand on their own as guiding forces for getting work done. Someone giving a presentation at work might be told to "keep things concise and short." That is more of a guideline than a process.

As a manager, should you consider developing a set of principles that will guide the work of your staff? Yes, I think so. I'd encourage you to make this a team activity. Brainstorm some work principles. Narrow down your brainstormed list to four or five principles that really emphasize the key aspects of how you want work to get done. After you have your list, test some of your process standards to ensure there is alignment between principles and standards.

One advantage of having these work principles explicit for your team is that, when there is uncertainty in a process, these principles can provide a kind of North Star for handling that uncertainty. For example, when a physician faces a new situation or uncharted medical territory, "first do no harm" is their North Star. Or in that fast-food restaurant, when things get hectic and the process might be a little out of control, remember to "be cheerful and appreciative." It is something—a performance standard of sort—that those frazzled workers can at least hang on to in that harried moment.

Preventative Measures and Contingency Measures

11

The rubber meets the road for process management when a manager layers into his or her process—at those key trouble spots—preventative and contingency measures. This is the heart of proactive process management. These measures or steps ensure the process does not falter and delivers as expected and promised.

Essentially, preventative measures and contingent measures are responses to two reasonable, forward-looking questions:

1. Has my team done a thoughtful job preventing the process from going off the rails?
2. Is my team prepared in case the process goes off the rails?

The difference between preventative and contingency measures might be best described by this simple car analogy. Preventative measures are like changing the oil in your car, assuming you don't own an electric car. You change the oil every so often to prevent the motor from damage due to overheating. Contingency measures are like the spare tire in your trunk. It is there just in case you need it. You may never use the spare, but it is there.

When talking with managers about process management, I often found that they already intuited the need for prevention and contingency and had already put some measures in place. Let's go back to our recruiting example. In an earlier chapter, we suggested that the fifth step—a slate of candidates presented—might be a problem step.

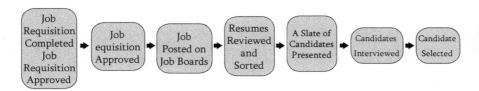

Job Requisition Completed Job Requisition Approved → Job equisition Approved → Job Posted on Job Boards → Resumes Reviewed and Sorted → A Slate of Candidates Presented → Candidates Interviewed → Candidate Selected

The root-cause analysis, you may recall, went like this:

And let's imagine that the troublesome step in this process is the fifth step—that about 40 percent of the time, the slate is weak and includes no great candidate worthy of hiring. Why is this happening?

First, we ask, what is working and what is not working. In this case, we'll say the previous four steps in the process are working (meeting standards), but the fifth step is not.

Second, we ask, Where is it working, and where is it not working? You ask your buddy over in another part of the company if she is having problems with her slates of candidates, and she says no. So, it is not working in your part of the business, but it is elsewhere.

Third, we ask, When was it working, and when was it not working? You note that this problem with weak slates began about six months ago. Prior to that, the slates were good.

Fourth, we ask, Who was involved when it was working, and who was involved when it was not working? You are the same hiring manager, so you are a constant. You note that seven months ago, a new recruiter was assigned to you, and that recruiter expanded the list of job boards used to create slates.

With just these four questions, we can narrow things down to two root-cause suspects: the quality of the recruiter and/or the quality of the job boards. With these in hand, you can investigate and remedy.

Let's say the conclusion is that the problem is the inexperience of the new recruiter. With that conclusion in mind, a preventative step might be that any new recruiter must share his or her proposed slates with a more experienced recruiter before sharing the slate with the hiring manager. This step might be a temporary step until a rookie recruiter builds capability and competence. Temporary or not, it is a preventative measure since it is trying to *prevent* a poor slate from being presented and wasting the hiring manager's time.

Could there have been a contingency step used alternatively for this situation? Since the presenting problem is so large (40 percent of the slates are unacceptable), a preventative measure makes more sense. But what if the presenting problem is smaller—say 1 percent rather than 40 percent? In this case, a contingency may be a reasonable alternative given the infrequency. You may recall that one of the customer standards for this process is keeping the cost per hire below $500. The manager of this process has probably focused on job boards that produce good candidates at a lower cost point. One contingent step here might be a more expensive, specialty job board kept available for moments when the standard boards do not yield enough good candidates. When a recruiter determines the slate is shaping up as weak, it triggers the use of the specialty job board—the contingency step. This step is invoked only if needed, but it is a forethought and not an afterthought. It is ready when needed.

When are contingent steps most valuable? Contingent steps are needed when a particular step in the process fails infrequently, but when it does fail, the efficacy of the whole process is at risk. Again, the spare tire is a nice metaphor. Are some steps in a process so critical that both a preventative and contingent measure are necessary? When the risks are really high—yes. NASA builds all sorts of redundancies into their protocols because, to borrow a phrase from the movie *Apollo 13*, "failure is not an option." Someone might call this a belts-and-suspenders approach to process management. Judge for yourself the need for such precautions in your processes. Collect the data, trust your experiences, and use common sense for any assumptions before pushing for redundant preventative and contingent measures.

> "Contingent steps are needed when a particular step in the process fails infrequently, but when it does fail, the efficacy of the whole process is at risk."

I want to emphasize one more time that not every step in a process needs an associated preventative or contingent measure—just those steps that regularly give you headaches or pose dramatic risk to the process.

Automation of processes has made inclusion of preventative and contingent steps almost invisible. When a hiring manager goes online to complete a job requisition, the system he or she uses will require certain fields to be completed before submission of the req can happen. This is a preventative measure that ensures all key information is inserted before moving on to the next step. Contingent steps can also be automated. For example, a certain hiring manager might have a budget limit on his or her payroll. If the submission of an electronic req for a new position happens to create a negative variance to the budget, an automated contingency step might be set up to flag the variance and redirect the hiring manager to a conversation with his or her manager before proceeding.

Once preventative and contingent measures are in place, the final two steps of the process of process management need to simply unfold.

The Process of Process Management

1. Know the process.
2. Set the standards.
3. Know the acceptable variances from standards.
4. Have a reporting mechanism for tracking variances.
5. Install preventative and contingency measures.
6. **Analyze the performance data regularly.**
7. **If negatively off variance, execute the contingency plans.**

Decide how often you need to see the process performance data (hourly? daily? weekly?) and use those reporting mechanisms you've installed to track that data. And if a step falters and it has a contingency plan, execute that plan. I can't resist pointing out that the seventh step in the process of process management is its own contingency step.

CHAPTER

12

Manager as Process and Productivity Coach

Managers have plenty of jobs, but I feel their primary job is to manage productivity. They have at their disposal a variety of resources to do this, including technology, machinery, tools, facilities, and money. And there are people and processes. This book has been about managing productivity by managing processes.

"Managers have plenty of jobs, but I feel their primary job is to manage productivity."

When we talk about managing people, we quickly identify the need for a manager to coach. Managers are sometimes career coaches or developmental coaches. They coach by giving feedback. They coach when they collaborate on the setting of someone's performance goals.

But there is also an opportunity for managers to think of themselves as process coaches, or people who help others work through their process responsibilities.

On the surface of it, a manager can coach someone through those seven steps in the process of process management. The manager might, for example, coach someone through the creation of a process map or the setting of process standards and targets.

But, as we have seen, there are deeper analytical skills being used in process management that managers can exploit as coaches. For example, the ladder of inference is a valuable framework for helping someone think through important decisions. As a process coach, calling on this tool to remind a staff member of the importance of data, experiences, assumptions, and beliefs can lead to not only better process decisions but also better decisions in general. The root-cause analysis framework of "what's working and what's not working" likewise has coaching value beyond process management. It could, for example, be used to assess why an employee who was previously a top talent in your group is suddenly performing poorly.

These are available productivity tools that can broaden a process coach into a full-fledged productivity coach. And there are plenty of other such tools out there. Here is a final one you might find useful. I referenced the book *The New Rational Manager* earlier when we were looking at the root causes of process trouble spots. In that book, the authors articulate a four-step process for critical thinking, which goes something like this:

o   First, size up the situation: what's wrong, what's right, and what are the opportunities?

o   Second, determine the root causes of the issues facing you—good or bad.

o   Third, set some criteria for a solution and pick the best solution or solutions.

o   Finally, make a plan and execute the decision.

Yes, I know this is pretty simple. But you'd be surprised how many times I have used this framework to coach someone working out a process issue. I have been shown processes by managers where it was clear that they had just slapped steps and standards into place without much thought. I coached them to step back from the process and do a situational scan of who their customers are, what those customers expect, and the track record of the process meeting those expectations. If the track record has been weak, what are some of the root causes that made it weak? This simple critical-thinking exercise, when well coached, can pay some valuable dividends.

Those dividends or productivity improvements are really the prize for any manager ready to attend to process management as thoughtfully as people management. So, don't be among those folks in my classes who say they aren't even sure what processes they own. Be among an apparently smaller group of managers who really know how to manage their processes.

Final Thoughts

13

Years ago, I read a management article titled "MacGregor" by Arthur Carlisle. It was a peculiar article because it was written sort of like a parable about leadership. I guess that's why it stuck with me. It was not your standard academic journal read. Some of the language in this article is now dated and shopworn, but its central message is timeless and relevant to process management. Plus, it is still a fun read.

MacGregor was the leader of an oil refinery. He ran one of many refineries in a larger oil and gas company. MacGregor's refinery happened to be the best in the company—the most productive and most profitable.

The article's message was very simple: if a leader can successfully delegate work to others, not only will the business thrive but everyone in the business will thrive as well. There is a lot of talk in the article about empowerment, accountability, feedback, and employee development. Most people who read it typically set the article down and reflect on its lessons about effective people management. That makes sense since the bulk of the article is about people-management issues.

But what some readers miss on their first pass is the importance MacGregor placed on process. MacGregor made it very clear that he had carefully constructed an operating process for his refinery that included clear standards, an effective reporting mechanism, some very clever preventative measures, and ready-to-go contingency plans. His belief was that without this operating process, he would be unable to effectively delegate and reap the benefits of that delegation. In his world, good process management made for good people management.

I drew this same conclusion early in my career. I suspect the managers at Harris Bank who raised the importance of process management to me years ago did the same.

> "When an employee asks the question, "What's expected of me?" the best answer to that question is likely rooted in well-managed processes where standards of performance are clear."

When an employee asks the question, "What's expected of me?" the best answer to that question is likely rooted in well-managed processes where standards of performance are clear. Process standards—both input and customer standards—inform the expectation of the employee's performance. Likewise, the answer to an employee's question, "How will I be rewarded?" is also related to those process standards. Employees are rewarded for meeting or exceeding standards. When preventative measures and contingency measures are in place, employees have a much better chance of getting their work done and meeting performance expectations.

This book is my way of making explicit what sometimes gets lost in the MacGregor article and I suspect might also have been glossed over in my first three books about people management. I'm not sure which is the chicken and which is the egg, but people management and process management are symbiotic tasks, both needing the balanced attention of those of us who have taken on management roles.

Or, putting it another way (and stealing from an earlier graphic) …

So, good luck in striking that balance.

Recommended Reading

I have found very few books that do a great job of integrating the topics of people management and process management. But here is one that did, and I recommend it if you want to explore more about these companion management responsibilities:

> Brockner, Joel. *The Process Matters.* Princeton University Press, 2016.

Here are two books I mentioned that were the source of content for the ladder of inference, root-cause analysis, and critical thinking:

> Senge, Peter. *The Fifth Discipline Fieldbook: Strategies and Tools for Building a Learning Organization.* Crown Business Publishing, 1994.
>
> Higgens Kepner, Charles, and Benjamin B. Tregoe. *The New Rational Manager.* Updated ed. Princeton Research Press, 1997.

This book focused on process management. But the basics of its close cousin, process improvement, should probably be understood by managers as well. Here is a nice, concise overview of process improvement you might find handy:

> Harvard Business Review. *Improving Business Processes.* Harvard Business Review Press, 2010.

And if that Harvard Business Review's book whets your appetite for full-scale business process management (sometimes referred to as BPM), here are two more serious editions focused on process improvement:

> Jeston, John. *Business Process Management: Practical Guidelines to Successful Implementations*. 4ᵗʰ ed. Routledge, 2018.
>
> Panagacos, Theodore. *The Ultimate Guide to Business Process Management: Everything You Need to Know and How to Apply It to Your Organization*. CreateSpace Independent Publishing Platform, 2012.

The MacGregor article I mentioned at the end of the book, along with a critique of it by its author, can be found be found in the August 1995 edition of *Organizational Dynamics Journal*, vol. 24. It is titled "MacGregor: An Organizational Dynamics Classic Revisited," and its author is Arthur Elliott Carlisle.

Carlisle also wrote a book that contains six business parables, one of which also explores the relations between process and people management:

> *Mac: Conversations about Management*. McGraw-Hill, 1983.

And since I reference my own book on team management, here it is:

> King, Steve. *Alignment, Process, Relationships: A Manager's Guide to Team Management*. Bloomington, IN: iUniverse, 2019.

About the Author

Steve King is the retired executive director for the Center for Professional and Executive Development at the University of Wisconsin's School of Business and the president of SDK Group, which specializes in helping organizations find solutions for their business-related talent-management issues.

Steve teaches at the University of Wisconsin–Madison, Northwestern University, and Morehouse College in Atlanta.

Steve spent more than twenty-five years leading in corporate settings. He was the senior vice president of Human Resources for Hewitt Associates, a global HR consulting and outsourcing firm. He also served as the vice president of global talent management for Baxter Healthcare; faculty leader for the Bank of Montreal's Institute for Learning in Toronto; and vice president of management and professional development for Harris Bank in Chicago.

Steve lives in Madison, Wisconsin, and is the author of three other books on management: *Brag, Worry, Wonder, Bet; Six Conversations;* and *Alignment, Process, Relationships.*

CPSIA information can be obtained
at www.ICGtesting.com
Printed in the USA
LVHW110421141021
700395LV00009B/796